The Algorithm
of I

Also by Jack Crocker

Poetry
The Last Resort

The Algorithm of I

00000110101
10001010101
11101101010
10111011010

JACK CROCKER

 MIMBRES PRESS
of Western New Mexico University

Mimbres Press of Western New Mexico University is dedicated to advancing the University's mission by publishing works of lasting value that reflect the intellectual, creative, historical, natural, and cultural heritage of the southwest region and state of New Mexico, as well as selective works of national and global significance.

FIRST EDITION, 2021
Request for permission to reproduce material from this work should be sent to:

Permissions
Mimbres Press
1000 W. College Avenue,
Silver City, NM 88061

Cover and Layout Design:
Paul Hotvedt, Blue Heron Typesetters, LLC

Photo Credit:
Jay Hemphill

Crocker, Jack, 1940–
The Algorithm of I / Jack Crocker.

ISBN - 978-163848324-3
LCCN - 2021909488

MIMBRES PRESS OF WESTERN NEW MEXICO UNIVERSITY
Western New Mexico University
P.O. Box 680
Silver City, New Mexico 88062

mimbrespress@wnmu.edu

To
Jodi, Jessi, and William
and

in memory of
Jessie Merle Knight Crocker
&
William Curtis Crocker

. . . If there is no past, there can be no self . . . .
Robert Penn Warren

. . . I think that it is a spiritual disaster to pretend that one doesn't love one's country. You may disapprove of it, you may be forced to leave it, you may live your whole life as a battle, yet I don't think you can escape it . . . .
James Baldwin

I feel related to the country, to this country, and yet I don't know exactly where I fit in . . . . There's always this kind of nostalgia for a place where you can reckon with yourself.
Sam Shepard

Maybe the human brain is an object beyond the reach of metaphor, for the simple reason that it is the only object capable of creating metaphors to describe itself. . . . [It] creates the human mind, then the human mind tries to understand the human brain, however long it takes and whatever the cost.
Luke Dittrich

CONTENTS

FOREWORD

Western New Mexico University is proud to publish Jack Crocker's *The Algorithm of I* as the first book of the newly formed Mimbres Press of Western New Mexico University. The press's mission is to publish works of lasting value that reflect the intellectual, creative, historical, natural, and cultural heritage of the southwest region and state of New Mexico, as well as selective works of national and global significance. Indeed, *The Algorithm of I* sets a very high bar for future publications to meet.

I am a mathematician which at first glance might suggest the opposite of a literary person and one not naturally suited to write a foreword for a book of poems. But then, mathematics is poetry in motion and when the book of poems is titled *The Algorithm of I*, it seems more appropriate.

I met Jack when we both were involved in the founding of Florida Gulf Coast University. For years we played golf together. He became a friend who challenged and mentored me into broader and deeper thinking. Through those times I learned details of his past. Now, through his poetry I have come to know more of his soul.

Raised on a farm in the Mississippi Delta of rich, alluvial soil that nurtured not only the cotton plant but also his early cultural identity, Jack found his voice while walking those dusty gravel roads and living his own Huckleberry Finn adventures. Jack's path to poetry began with a voice like Elvis, and an early temptation to have a musical career, starting with songwriting. Later in life he would sign a recording contract with Fretone Records in Memphis. Equally compelling were a blazing fastball with a curveball "painting the corners of the plate" and his high arc basketball shot landing sweetly in the net pulling him toward college where he received scholarhips in both sports. But it was youthful love that moved him toward education, a shift in values, and eventually to poetry in its purest form.

The Algorithm of I is a reflective journey of intellectual prowess that spins nostalgia with purpose and wonders about life, faith, and human evolution. It reflects Jack's journey of self-examination incorporating his influences and influencers. It questions chance, randomness, and the universe itself. The writing is both blissfully beautiful and subtle. It transcends the era of Jack's physical journey to the culmination of the ultimate journey of inward thought and consciousness that makes us human.

The events of the 1960s shaped Jack when Vietnam and civil rights challenged southern thinking and tradition. His values were formed by education and later by the ability to leave the Delta and witness different viewpoints and places far from the Southern world. Jack's journey is one that was guided by pursuing education, sharing knowledge, and ultimately fueled by love. His poetry reflects a life that leads him to challenge the very brain that guided his path beyond the cotton fields of his youth.

Of our golfing foursome, I was the only one with children at the time. Jack was always interested in my children's growth, but I felt he did not fully understand what fatherhood was truly about. I share this because Jack's poem of life was about to be radically changed.

In 2004 Jack began courting a beautiful woman who bore him two wonderful children: Jessi and William. The evolution of Jack's conversation with his brain dramatically shifted to an understanding of what love and sacrifice ultimately meant. As he moved through middle age the contemplation of death and the avoidance of it became a major theme, for now he had found the continuation of life through his children.

With aging, one of the mind's challenges is to come to terms with the body's decline. Jack's athletic legacy is overshadowed particularly by the experience of having young children. And so this book is his Olympic marathon of memory and intellect where the mind shows the body what can be done when the body is no longer as willing. In the end the *The Algorithm of I* becomes the algorithm of life—as well as a significant and distinguished beginning for the birth of the Mimbres Press of Western New Mexico University.

Joseph Shepard, President
Western New Mexico University

ACKNOWLEDGMENTS

Deep and wide thanks go to those who helped make this book possible: Joe Shepard for his friendship and vision to establish the Mimbres Press of Western New Mexico University; long-time existentialist "brother" and teammate Larry Broer, whose reading of the poems always revealed more than I knew was there; writer, scholar, and musician friends Herb Karl, Dick Dietrich, and Chuck Heaton who kept me humble; D. C. Berry, master poet and metaphor maker who slashed a few poems for brevity and bragged on rime; JJ Amaworo Wilson, whose sensitive and intelligent editing made the poems better; Valerie Plame and Marvel Harrison for organizing and setting the foundation for the Mimbres Press and sweet encouragement to meet deadlines; Paul Hotvedt, not only for the artistry of design but also patience with my creative self-doubt and rewrites; Mary Wallace, for understanding the expatriation; and Jodi, Jessi, and William—the continuing reasons to write and to wake up every morning. I am forever grateful and honored for The Algorithm of I to be the inaugural publication of the Mimbres Press of Western New Mexico University.

PROLOGUE

If I could break away and just be,
Become like a stone in a flowing stream,
Or join the wind, gain reprieve, absolved
Of the I that's me, would love remain?
Guilt still sting? The exits of pretend exist?
The heat of desire against another's skin?
Would wonder starve into the grave of what is?
Risk step back from pleasure's cliffs?
Voice go silent and language disappear?
Roots of place relinquish connection?

When my brain and I come to rest in frustration
From chasing the secrets of itself, I choose
Not some garden of transcendent isolation,
But nature's thickets of thought and intuition
Where mind and I hunt with human words
And animal sensation metaphors like trophies
For the walls of empty pages.

OFFERING

I did not exist without them and you
And then us at the breast of a world local
With names in the infinity of space and time—
The weathered house in a cotton field,
Off a gravel road that led to everywhere—
All the places I was ignorant of. First, only
The joy at your breast with nothing to do
But begin to know, not even I yet, just
The random explosion, the little big bang,
The atom dispersal that made me a singular
Universe, the quantum splash that set in
Motion the journey to entropy, the gravitational
Waves moving from the center of the generous
Brine to deliver me into the Mississippi Delta,
The sharecropping struggle of the haves
And have nots, learning the mule's way to
Step between rows, lessons Bilboed in like
Weather, the land all seed and black soul,
And the white residue of alluvial dreams
Forced apart but strung together.
The waves flow closer to shore, each orbit
A life of the center, over depths of desire and
Uncertainty, through successive exits toward
Not redemption but acceptance of purposeless
Stars on winter nights, to end up here at the
Anthropocene, devising ways of gratitude in
The short time left to walk back down the hill
To the stone, time enough to imagine victory
And offer the ashes of a few poems.

The Algorithm
of I

THE ALGORITHM OF I

If chance is the companion of birth, is birth the ancestral
Prison where the brain arranges the "I" of self? And freedom
From the random sentence of life is found only in death?

Can we make glorious the art of joy and grief, proclaim
Victory—not in the promised rewards of myth—but breath
By breath in daily revolt—step by completed step?

I suppose "I" interrogating the brain is the tail chasing
The cat. After all, I'm locked in its cells of being.
(Can the 1s and 0s trapped in its folds and troughs

Trick me into believing I'm free?) Or, Ventriloquist,
Is it telling me what to say, just as the spiral chains
Of the double helix shackled me from the beginning?

Yet, how does the brain explain the mind? Is it a
Rogue angel exiled from the cerebellum but allowed to
Pal around with its buddies in the playground of the

Neocortex? Is the enfant brain like a jukebox, preloaded,
Until the mind kicks in—tuning in to a new playlist,
Singing its own songs, dancing to a different beat?

And then there's gut feeling—an intuitive spark
That catches the brain looking the other way? And
All the organs that serve emotions, the irascible spleen

And glorious heart—the fertile cause of love and all
Its fallible effects (not to forget the exalted private parts
And whatever explodes when beauty is perceived).

Did reason come first, or faith? Perhaps once upon a time
A committee of brains failing to reason themselves out of
Death spread the tale of eternal life to save face and keep

Power with faith for savior against doubt. (Knowledge
Pitted god against man. Animal nakedness was lost to
Shame. Sacrifice became the cost of salvation and nations

Surrendered to the pulpit conspiracies of fear.) (Or, is this
The brain's power play to hide responsibility in the rule of those
Who cannot reason beyond the utility of religion?)

(And faith is the spiritual mantra the neurons make, the brain's
Choir, harmonizing to the big bang frequency of the universe?)
I don't know how out of our chemical innocence guilt came, but it's

Kin to spirit and soul—ghosts the brain gives as pablum
For the unexplainable? Are the neuron glitches that gave us
Mozart and serial killers random, or of the same intent?

Why is the brain so defensive about itself? Dining on
perceptions and sunning on the algorithm of need, does it
Amuse itself with hints and labyrinthine leads, partial truths

And dead ends? Is it afraid of its alien siblings gestating
In the lab-wombs of god-brains creating a new digital Eden? Or
Is it addicted to its own self-deception, distracting itself

From the only word that completes the sentence of life?
Lately, it's letting itself be called a predictive error machine.
(I still answer no to the robot question, though captchas give

Me grief.) Entertaining perhaps, but doing battle with
The brain I can't win. Programmed between the contradiction
Of predestination and hubris of free, there's one last

Trick to play: I turn to imagination, the sweetest dream
That thinking knows, and stand mentally naked before
The mirror of I am, was, and cannot help but be:

Cell
A genetic comma surviving the tidal pool
Translations of nature's phrases.

Primitive
Married to the universe in a union of senses
Until consciousness fell in love with itself.

Homo sapiens
Moving across trade routes of survival
Exchanging Neanderthal genes.

Human
Learning to sign my own name against
The power of systems that would sign for me.

Male
Arrogantly posing as the climax
Of evolutionary intent.

Hunter
Raised by the rifle,
Outgrowing the nature to kill.

Athlete
Tracing the arc of instinct toward
The void of the eternal hoop.

Believer
Accepting that gods do not exist
Except in the need for belief.

Atheist
Reasoning with the passion of faith that heaven
And hell exist only as hope and fear.

Individualist
Putting new tattoos
On old arms of tradition.

Citizen
Living in the social soup of custom and cant
Voting on which spoon to use.

Existentialist
Taunting the absurd by stopping for snacks
On the way back down to where the boulder waits.

Capitalist
Descending the high-rise of profit
To where enough is getting ahead.

Consumer
Cajoled by cleavage to invest in dreams—
A new pair of cowboy boots the only gain.

Taoist
Dissolving self in burning sage to breathe
The vapors of Yin and Yang.

Musician
Planted in Country, rooted in Blues,
Branched out in Rock-n-roll.

Gambler
Shooting the dice of orgasms
In the roulette beds of one-night-stands.

Dreamer
Going to sleep with scripts
Of unreal possibilities . . . .

Realist
Firmly ignorant of much,
Skeptical of the truth of truths.

Hedonist
Thinking vomit reveals the inner life
Of last night's binge.

Delusionist
Lured to the comfort of convenient lies
When scraps of truth are not enough.

Optimist
Lifting to vertical each morning
Knowing death is the only thing we own forever.

Pessimist
Leaving a light on at night,
To mimic counterfeit eternity.

Insomniac
Sweat-awakened at 3:00 a.m. to the hounds of terror
Unleashed into the future's urgency.

Anemic
Believing words are vitamins
To hold decomposition at bay.

Rhetorician
Slick-tongued agent of language
Pulling joy out of the hat of grief.

Artist
Devising gifts of light in exchange
For the dark promise of empty canvases.

Lover
From the first touch of Lynda Boykin's lips
Addicted to the fate of female mercy.

Husband
Hell was Baptist for those who would not wait.
Marriage, then, was the heaven of lust.

Mississippian
Suffering the 2016 election,
Emmett Till exhumed to be killed again.

Southerner
Birth by chance battling the birthmark of
A past that lives in the future again and again.

Hiker
Using trailheads for entry as next
Of kin into Nature's reunions.

Environmentalist
Moved to mountains from the apocalyptic beach,
As if altitude could prevent catastrophe.

Seeker
Neuronal collisions with truth
At the crossroads of beliefs and dreams.

Scholar
Not of footnotes and learned critiques,
But receptor of feelings, mentor of thought.

Tourist
Believing anonymity of place
Is a way to learn the lies of maps.

Wino
Uncertified sommelier of soil and sun,
Addict of the grape's momentary truth.

Alien
Gravity-browsing the boulevards
Of galactic neighborhoods.

Historian
Staring through the window's reflections
To imagine what the panes have seen.

Philosopher
Of black holes schooled in darkness
Of the mind seeking the light of pretend.

Futurist
Imagining beyond the present's cage
As far as the past can see.

Poet
Pushing the limits of words
To go beyond what they are.

Father
Love, finally, asking forgiveness from Jessi and Will
For coming so late to Jodi.

00011000001100101011001011111011011000
10000001010011001001101101011000000110
0000011010110 **EXPATRIATE** 1011010101011
10110101011100101010110100001011110001
00011000001100101011001011111011011000

HOME PLACE

The house has stood empty fifteen years.
I've returned each summer for the peace I feel
Watching it lean against the absence
Of those who brought it to life.
I walk around it silently and think
I hear the sigh of nails ungrip, letting
The weary rafters and studs pull away
To gravity and the whims of wind.
The circumference of fence is a faint hint.
A few snaggled posts remain,
Useless fangs weathered and veined
Like the final years of my father's skin.
It has held its ground as the tractors cut
The rows as close as they could get
To the front steps and side porch
That looks out yet on the seasons' swing.
I could rent it out, just as I do the land,
But I prefer its future unlived, no thoughtless
Breaths fouling the space or strange feet
Disturbing the floors my grandfather laid.
I let it stand, crypt and museum,
Until the fire came. I took four charred
Bricks, a single disc blade, a faceplate,
And a scorched Old Grandad whiskey flask—
A leftover sin the flames unhid.
Now it's an unmarked grave, all remnants
Bulldozed beneath the ground to free up
Another acre or two to be tilled.
Today I stand like a headstone where
The front steps were, feeling the memorial
Peace of vacant air, purified by fire,
The only movement my mind, ticking,
The way a watch holds time.

THE VISIT

The road to where I was born is dying.
The farm-to-market asphalt rotting away
To its gravel bones. Mr. Bingham, the Mannings,
The Smiths, Boykins, Daniels, went long ago.
Where the asbestos-shingled house stood
No fence posts or mailbox is left to signal home.
All welcome has vanished, even the banquet
Of pecan trees, and the oak's summer shade.

Gray knots of sparrows stitched along the power lines
Bid no recognition and fly away as I have done.
Nothing is left but the plowed land, fallow now,
Fertile with time and harvest free.

It is here at the end of this waiting row
Where my father would ponder how deep
The cotton seeds should go, a ritual of faith
In the meteorology of harvest hope.

I am here where I once was,
Homeless and free to go.

EXIT

I left
before
I left,
doubts
rising
like vapors
off
the bayous
the slave
took
to escape
the dogs.
I hid
in the
contradiction
between
Jesus
and the sermons'
bark
and found
the exit
on the other
side
of my father's
walls.

THE MIRROR

The receding hairline pulls
My father's face over mine,
The broad forehead cloudless
Before the weather of pain set in.

Is he watching me take the mound
And with hawk accuracy call
Strike every time my curve ball
Paints the corners of the plate?

Or grinning at my soiled skin,
The refugee of threshing storms
In his ripe field of wheat
And my brooding plot of dreams?

Or remembering the sure arc
Of my hoop fame that brought
Home the trophies from local
Games and a college scholarship?

Or, is that what I see—
The reflection of reflections?

Is he watching my prodigal face
Turned away from the homestead
Beliefs, slowly disappearing into
The vanishing point where the rails

Meet? In his eyes is that oblique
Regret written by his hand
In the one letter he sent? Across the miles
I found it yesterday in the few things

I keep. After mention of the crops I
Could feel the pen lift, before the words
Came: We know you live a different life
But send you our prayers. God bless.

Or were those my sister's words?
The bible verses she underlined accepted
Forgiveness without blame. The only prayer
My father made was for rain.

And I see in his face, my face, that prayer's
Truth, the reality of survival and fertility
Of the land. The church was in his breast
Where kindness flourished even in drought.

This is the last face I see, called back
After his blood rebelled, the pain I watched
Transfusion after transfusion until his heart
Failed. At the end I saw. And now,

Through our Janus face I know the entrances
And exits of the blood our hearts share.

YAHRZEIT MOON

Memory makes your absence real
To see you again so primly propped,
A life of giving given out, posing
In full possession of nothing but love.

Tonight's moon moves in the moonlit
Absence as then, the stars like dim lit tears,
Night netting the spring oak, every
Leaf a tongue of grief.

As spring revives the beauty of death,
You return in serial resurrection,
Womb of beginning and end,
My inheritance of love and anger.

WHEN YOUR FATHER DIES
TAKE NOTES
SOMEWHERE INSIDE

Miller Williams

The side porch, a waiting room,
Is unusually warm for December.

Through the screen wire the moon
Carries a cross up the night.

Wind jangles fallen leaves like nerves
Shaking loose pocket change.

Through the window I see you picking
Something from the empty air,

Something you never reached in life,
Or a memory running away.

A new silence surrounds the bed.
You give up and are still.

The moon snags on a bare limb
And the night bleeds.

DEATH IS THE MOTHER OF PIES

Neighbors and aunts felt funerals
In the kitchen rather than the brain.
Celebratory in the voracious hunger

Of loss, they converged in the house
Where the coffin lay, Tupperware
Gorged with grief's smorgasbord

Of desserts, fried chicken, and vegetable
Trays, as if death's unslakeable
Appetite could be appeased.

I liked Aunt Nora's coconut pie
The best, white gold shredded into
A sugared egg and vanilla cream

Crowned by a cloud of heavenly
Meringue that God Himself would
Push you aside to taste.

On that day when a slice was served
To me on my mother's china plate
The glut of want was dead.

That day any bite I would take was like
The rite of feeding the ready mouth
And empty belly of the grave.

A GOOD MAN

The Middle Passage never died,
Only turned into double chains.
Once bought, the owned became
Owner of the master's claims
To superior race and every deed
Had to stand the test of the inhumane
Clenched fist of violent control.
Even his compassionate heart and soul

Could not dismiss the misstated tone,
The gasoline insult the question raised:
"I think that cost is wrong, Mr. Curt."
In his world there was no surprise,
The blow was unintended even to hurt,
Just the match struck on the stone
Sacrament of being white,
No thought of being wrong or right.

THE PATERNALISM OF CORN

Clucking as if with gratitude
The chickens gave offerings of eggs and a chosen
Few their necks, wrung, to serve as Sunday
Dinners when the preacher came.

And when the weather was right
One pig from those happy on fermented mash
Gave itself for a year's supply of pork--
The food chain etiquette of proper slaughter:
Step 1: prepare knives and saw;
Step 2: heat the water;
Step 3: .22 rifle shot to the brain;
Step 4: (Touch the eye. If it blinks shoot again.)
Step 5: Exsanguinate and hang the carcass;
Step 6: Scald and scrape the skin bare;
Step 7: (If barrow cut the penis.)
Step 8: Eviscerate from the anus down.
Step 9: Split the carcass and rinse,
Step 10: carve for the winter months ahead.

The chosen steer followed the pig's rite,
With the added humiliation of castration.
(Sometimes in distant thunder I hear again
The thud the sledgehammer made, the violent
Shiver, and the front legs folding to kneel
As if in obeisance to its corn-fed fate.)

At noon the field hands, unshackled
From the cotton sack straps scarring their backs
With plantation history, would rise off their knees
And cross the gravel road to my father's country store,
Wait in humble queue, to be taken care of
With pig's feet, ham hocks, beef stew,

And fried chicken my mother made to feed
My farm-raised survival.

Here's my menu: I lived off a roux of love with sauces
Of pain, violent hors d'oeuvres, and bitter desserts--
To chew now on a dose of childhood truth.

CONVERSATION WITH A CONFEDERATE STATUE

Your rifle, leaf-checkered, moves
In the autumn light as if ready to fire.
It is my mind that swerves—
Eyes catching shadow. A bier

Is all you are when leaves are still,
Progeny of the sculptor's hand,
Inert matter, deaf to the bugle's call,
Bronzed in the act of attack and defend.

Though kin to your history's cause
I laid down arms long ago,
And live not in the shadow of was
But the light of letting go.

The forklift of streaming history
Hooks, like symbol to symbol,
The gaunt warrior,
Adamant on his pedestal
Of weaponed memory.
In his face the unrepentant price
Of loss preserves the communion of valor
That transmutes the blood sacrifice
Into fervent readiness to rise once more.

I watch the simple hydraulic
Force lift and lower the hollow
Cause slowly to the ground.
And know it's only symbolic,
Not the death of the hallowed
State of mind taken down.

The people who put it up
Did not cross the Pettus Bridge
Or write a letter from the Birmingham jail.
They did summarily acquit,
With defiance that savors outrage,
The smiling killers of Emmett Till.

The statue is not dead, just gone
To a different location, its future still
A veneration of the past.
The myth remains carved in stone—
Provides the political swill
That sustains the caste
White power depends upon.

Now malice spread from the Whitest House
Released the hemophilia of the lost cause—

Enslaved history is not the South's alone,
But genetic repetition replayed in the course
Of our lives, a generation to generation clone.

In this dark time of broken vows
What will come to break the natural laws?

MIGRATION

He steps out for milk to walk
The few blocks of the concrete field
Where nothing grows but debt
Planted in the market seeds of want,
And remembers what he left.

By now the crops will be zipped
And swelling inside the same acres
Under the same moon that makes
The sleeping cows look like a crop
Of stones. The old man is slumped
Asleep in his chair, each sharing
Comfort of the other's sag, his unlaced
Shoes fertilizing the hooked rug,
His sweat nightcooled, the *Delta
Farm Press* napkined across his
Lap. The same hand will shake
Him to bed, the dishes done.

He carries this across the traffic
Into the bright convenience of easy
Transactions, and walks back the
Other side of the street to the house,
Or one like it, where home is
Always someplace else.

ANCESTRY

How strange it seems to hold history in my
      Mouth, the saliva chronicles taking me
By way of Scotland, Norway, Wales, England
      And Northwest Europe
On a migrant journey across the Atlantic
      To end up in Paris, Mississippi, where
A grist mill on the Yocona River would feed
      My clan long enough to plant a cemetery with my
DNA. (It adds expectorant meaning
      To "spit it out," as my father used to say
To get at whatever lie I was choking on.)
      I can accept I came out of mud, was brother
To bonobos and ended up in the linear descent
      Of Solomon Crocker marching into the regal
Lines of Redcoat muskets, and kin to Private Arthur
      Martin's abiding myth, handed down
In a closed loop, getting killed over and over again
      Following Pickett into the blue death
Of Cemetery Ridge. Myths escape the truth
      The double helix tells and belief is not dependent
On blood. I have bible-thumping cousins who would
      Send me to Hell for not believing what they sell.
What hurts is that I have to go on living
      With the diminished truth that Grandma Knight
Was Choctaw is a lie.

FIRST LUST

Growing up I was taught the path to follow
Was laid out by the Gentile Jesus
Crudely painted above the baptism pool,
The crown of thorns more like a beauty
Queen tiara. Two roads, graveled with fear,
Diverged into an everlasting wood:
Down was bad. Up was good.

Until about 12 I was a good little fellow,
Made my bed, mowed the yard, didn't cuss,
Took seriously lessons of sin in Sunday school.
And then my penis became aware of Becky
Fowler. I stopped closing my eyes in prayer
To stare, leer, even though I knew the Lord
Was watching and taking notes of my lewd

Behavior and naked thoughts, too callow
To know the glandular heat of rising lust.
But now I vow that abstinence is cruel.
If Hell leads me down the path of Becky
Fowlers, I go believing love and desire
Are echoes of yearning, the animal Code
That keeps us human—nature's God.

The pasture sleeps and the graveled road becomes
A dark ribbon of exit.
Tree frogs beg for mates.
Cotton roots sip the sandy soil to feed the lusty bolls.
Fifteen miles away
Clarksdale glows in its milky rendezvous
With the night
Where cheerleaders cheer
The testosterone violence of teenage
Boys baptized in the glory of bootleg beer.
The last night of revival
Churns up guilt
In the hard Baptist pews and
With all heads bowed and all eyes closed
Just as I Am prolongs the last seductive chance
For lost sinners to walk into
The loving arms of faith.
The moon praises the trees and irrigated with
Dreams
The night blooms into vague desire.

In three more years I will stand at the crossroads
Of 61 and 49 and make my Robert Johnson deal.

ELVIS

It's midnight in a '58 Ford
And I'm doing Maybeline's
Hunnerd and four, my souped-up
Heart racing to Red Hot and Blue,
Blood tuned to the DNA of WHBQ
And Dewey "Anybody Wanna
Buy a Duck!" Phillips,
The only white man spinning
The soul of blues, born in
The gospel womb of Delta dirt
And the juke joints of Saturday
Night sin, hormones harmonizing
In the key of E, twelve bars of
Puberty rocking in on the Midnight
Special and thrust of Elvis hips,
Learning fast a Stella guitar,
Gut-bucket growl, and snarling lip
Would get me the long tall sally
Beat of backseat thrills.

MAIL FANTASIES

On rural route one, rain or shine, the mailbox
Mothered my dreams like a womb of hope.
I believed in its umbilical fantasies (never a hoax!)
Like a fervent evangelical told by the Holy Ghost
To expect the Rapture to arrive with the next frost.
 I did not rule out even a visit from the Pope.

"DEAR WILLIAM, as you know we are still
Mourning the tragic death of Clayton Moore.
But the play must go on. After viewing thousands
Of masked faces, our talent scout has chosen
YOU to audition for the new LONE RANGER.
 Soon, we will send you further instructions regarding
Travel and dates. The enclosed SILVER BULLET will
Get you through the gate. Tonto and Scout are excited
To meet you and send CONGRATULATIONS.
Until then, HI HO SILVER, AWAY!

CONGRATULATIONS, WILLIAM! Your heartfelt
Letter of adulation has won the contest to meet
Lash Larue! You will join him at the annual
Quitman County Fair in October where he will
By rousing demand once again unfurl his famous
Black Mamba Whip to flick the cigarette
From Busty LaMont's lips. YOU will light the
Cigarette and take the butt-end from her mouth
After the Black Mamba has snuffed it out.
Specific date and time will be coming soon.
The spotlight is on YOU!

Faith fulfilled can be a surprise. A new sacred book
Astounded a mailbox prayer, like mislabeled contraband.
In brightly colored pages Busty posed (dare to look!)
Sparingly dressed. Then, at night, the moon leering
Through my window, she began to slip into my lingerie
Dreams, cigarette lit, my whip in hand.

LEVITATION

The hoop is nailed
        To the smoke house wall,
Too high and too close for lay-ups.
        In magic levitation
I take jump shot after
        Jump shot, intervals from earth
Where dreams can breathe.
        I shoot until dark.
On full moon nights the eternal circle
        Doubles. The arcing
Globe is perfect. Nothing but net.
        The fields gather around me,
Centered, selfless, full of emptiness,
        The pureness
Of a buck clearing a barbed-wire fence.

GET WELL

We called him Duck for his face and gait.
At five eight, with athletic heart, he fed
Me the ball, me, I, the shooter of renown.

At times I dream of his scrappy defense against
The radiation assault and chemo-aggression,
Setting screens for my first scrimmage with death.

I was not aware the forced smile and weak hand
Were goodbye until the funeral came.
In alien mourning I joined the ceremony of sorrow.

How much of public grief is show?
The very next day my life was whole.

SCHOOL DAYS

Looking back to see
myself coming I go
to the first grade picture:

Hair:
slicked back,
unnaturally tamed;

Smile:
on its way
but not there yet;

Arms:
folded, heart shield,
self-embrace;

Eyes:
already wary,
photographing the camera.

GRAMMAR

I spoke early
mother said,
but I'm not sure
when I discovered
the life of words.
I remember needing
them to make
a silhouette of sad.
I learned the future
can spring from one—
like door, bigotry,
kiss.

RITUAL

It was the coldest dawn
I had felt. Twelve years old,
Statued on my assigned stand,
So cold I hugged the 20-gauge,
My first real weapon toward
Being a man. Edging to the sun's
Recognition I broke the first rule:
Be still and let the buck come
To you. Even the dogs' belling
Seemed to hang like icicles in the
Brightening canopy of trees.
Then it happened, the blood boil
Of a buck turning sideways to take
My double-ought slug to the heart.
The blur of fire in my lungs; the camp
Celebration; trophy gutted; my father's
Pride; paying homage to the herd;
Rubbing on my face the blood, spirit
To spirit, war paint of my first kill.
For me the blood has stayed. I went
Out as a child, came back as Cain.

SPRING

I remember
the jonquils.
They lit up
the front yard
with the color
of hope when
life was forever.

The bright
breaths of air
are still there
and the fresh
hovering sky,
and like eternal
yellow magnets
they pull
beauty all
around them
in the place
where the
house
no longer stands.

WINTER

I like winter,
not as a lover
but a close friend—
morning frost
and the stiffened
air of twilight,
and then snow:
the small print
of fall erased;
the promise
of spring
put on hold.

000110000011001010110010111110110110001
100000010100110010011011101011000000110
0000011010110 **A NEW PLACE** 101101010101
110110101011100101010110100001111110001
000110000011001010110010111110110110001

FEEDING THE BIRDS

I refill the feeders and watch the birds return,
Three courageous scouts exploring the bounty.
Soon the word is out. The sparrows are first
And then a rush of nervous titmice flutter in
And out. Blustery doves bully the air. Gambel's
Quail sneak in by ground to the seed block stand.
I stretch out in bed to read and suddenly think
Of the monk who lay in his coffin each morning,
Rehearsing.
A breeze through the open door
Takes me back to our time living on the beach,
The wide water bright in the morning, fading
To black hole at night, a ship's light floating like
A star on the horizon. Sudden storms brought
The damp urgency of desire.
                    Now we are among the mountains,
The Gila range—farther west where the sun's
Light is delayed (though higher, I'm no further
From the grave). We refill our lives with fate more
Than plan. Today, while you and the kids are out
Buying milk and bread, I watch the avid beaks tick
The grain away, and listen to the birds sing us into
Our new place. Tomorrow, I'll fill the feeders again.
Love works that way.

DRIVING THE BLACK RANGE

At Kingston the sprint begins, the need
    To compete against the mountains' challenge,
Breathing the atmosphere of height,
    Leaning into the serpentine
        Curves of passage.

It's the internal combustion engines' hell
    And the marathon test of nerves against time's
    Switch-back record
        To top the peak, assault
    The descent, and then flatten-out
In the Mimbres Valley to bring life level again.

But slow down, slow down,
    See what is missed:

On the high south slope the fire spirit lingers
    Black among the charred ponderosa pines,
        Spiking the ridge like a porcupine's back.
In the sun's slant there's green again
        Scrub oak
    And colonies of young aspen
        Rise
    Out of the regenerating earth
        In verdant resurrection.

At Emory Pass stop, get out, broaden your gaze.
    How sublime the theatrical space that lies
    In the valley's lap! From here
        The plot takes hold:
    The iridescent crow
    Clacks and rattles its discordant caws.

In burrows, lairs, nests, tunnels, dens—-
       In the sanctuaries of primordial time—-
       The algorithm
            Of Nature unfolds.
The hare feeds the hawk. The great horned owl
       Serenades its prey.
       Elk graze the gramma grass.
   Deer bed down in the tall fescue
            Hidden
From the primal aim of the hunter's eye.

   Descend
       We must, but slow,
       Slow,
       Stop.
Imagine the eagle's view.
Look back at what the mountains gave.
       And pause
For the brief moment it takes
       To become one
With the fragment of eternity we are passing through.

CAMPING OUT

for Dennis

We went beyond
The internet's reach
To the box canyon of Mogollon Creek

And pitched our tents beneath
The acne-skinned sycamores
Shading us as if they cared—

Kindness nevertheless—
A loveliness our eyes came
To accept.

Beside us the Gila knows
Where it is going. We hear
It greet a colony of stones

And pass on, the sound
We humans have tried to ape
With the word *susurration.*

Cottonwoods feast on its flow,
It feeds the sycamores and all
The needy things

Along its walls, even
The sinister green
Of the exotic cedars.

A line of downcast
Willows weep like spurned suitors
At the river's always leaving.

The dry creek sleeps
Lonely in its flowing bed
Of rocks waiting like memories

For the monsoon storms.
(Yet, there is beauty
In despair and the cycle of being.)

We have reached a place
To slow down,
Pulled only by the speed

Of stars across the still
Vastness of the studded sky,
To lie cocooned

In the belly of our tent
Listening to the night wind
Tolling fall through the leaves.

(Winter is north of us,
A distance, for now,
Not to be reckoned with.)

At dawn light breaks
Over the mountain ridge
And reborn we stack a pyramid

Of kindling to spark fire
In a circle of stones, warding off
The spirits of morning chill.

For a while we convalesce
In the web of being,
As if in a dream

We have paused
Time to reenact the eternal
Blessings of natural intent.

Tomorrow we face
Tomorrow's truth:
We pack up and leave.

A single forsythia centers the universe
Yellow—
Pulls down the sky in blue adoration.
Tonight, the quarter moon will smile
With pleasure and stars linger to gawk.
On the other side of the yard the dull
White apricot cannot compete.
With seeds enwombed it bides its time
For the ripe honor its gifts receive.

I sit amused in this cosmic scene—
A congregation of atoms sipping
Another vodka tonic, actor
Musing over the script. Has valiant
Autumn taken a knee and handed
Its dulled winter sword to me?
Am I the director spirit of spring?
A priest of galactic glory, aided by
The spiritual courage of distilled maize?

The universe gives no credit for vision,
Nor praise for metaphors turned to song,
Or sense of humor to applaud the absurd.

The forsythia came to me, and I
To it, relatives in a photon collision
Where only light is constant and the mystery
Of beauty and truth lives in the explosion.

If Nature lets me stage the universe,
Knowledge makes me owner of thought.
I know the yellow blaze will dim
And die, turn to ashes of snow
In thoughtless preparation to enthrall

With yellow once again. And I'll wait—
An evolving carcass of cellular hope.

I'll come to the yellow again to play
With the stars, and until the final season
Of chaos comes the battered atoms
Of my heart will go on arranging themselves
In the possibility of human love, and revolt.

OWL NIGHT

Five nights a curious old owl,
An insomniac fool of a fowl
Kept awake an undying doubt
With its constant questioning howl
That drove me to seek it out.

Sleep-walking but waxing awake
I sloshed through a marshy brake
With drowsy steps in stumbling stealth
To the tree and moonlit lake
And stared up wise-eyed at myself.

GIMME THE BEAT. . . .

It's the beginning of fall: leaves
Chime in the wind and waver letting go.

I dance this littering waltz in time
To the lingering grace of hope

To hear the music of the roots,
The music that makes the grass shake

And the wind applaud the moves
To which I must believe we

Once were attuned—when we danced
With the trees and animal kin

To the rhythm of rain and joy of rivers
Humming through mountain and plain.

Again, the leaves begin to flower the ground
Like winter promises of spring, and today

I rejoice in the universal jig of the food chain,
Letting go, drifting away.

ARISING

There's a suddenness that comes with age
When you and the sun break sleep together.
The abrupt release from a drowsy cage
Of dreams dissolves into another
Startling day. Light arrives.
The original particles and waves of time
Bring the dawning archives
Of history for me to imagine

Once again there's meaning in the leaves
The juniper presents through the latticed
Net of the iron fence, the double weave
Like spiraled genes a Monet has laced
Together into a blurred canvas of belief:
We live in the art of joy and grief.

00011000001100101011001011111011011000
10000001010011001001101101011000000110
0010001101101110 **LESSONS** 10110101010111
01101010111001010101101000010111100001
00011000001100101011001011111011011000

CHURCH

In the fourteen section woods I found
A grove of walnut, hickory, and oak,
A Stonehenge clearing, chapel serene,
Where I would ride, dismount, and sit
Silent as moss to let the mystery in.
The fabulous light filtered through the leaves
Linked me to what is, and I came to know
That holiness has nothing to do with sin.

QUANTUM MECHANICS

The coin flip landed on purpose
So I played that game scrimmaging
On a field of meaning, as if someone

Was keeping score. I ask with Frost
If design is so small in the spider's art
Is the game played beyond the law?

Hearing no answer from the sky
I went out into the dark matter
Of the universe to look at Crane's

High cold star on a winter's night
And flipped the coin again
To play the odds.

A CHILD'S GAME

It's the third time in 76 miles
Jessi has asked, "Are we there yet?"
It's a profound question.

ANIMAL SENSE

Flicker did not like the saddle,
Even the small one that fit me.
I learned the language of her eyes,
The left eye biting me at the last
Tug of the cinch. Mounted inside
The barn she bucked my head
Against the rafters and raked me
To the ground. She walked to the open
And waited, looked at me then
Looked away— teacher:
This is the way the world is.

DOVE FIELDS

The dove has two eyes . . . With one it
foresees things to come; with the other it weeps
over what has been.

The Aberdeen Bestiary

i.

Deacons and derelicts ring the little valley
Of harvested grain to shoot the virtuous doves
Whose fame for peace the bible has acclaimed.
In the leading aim to birdshot death they
Fall like grey clumps of melting hail.
No timeout is taken to repent.
De-feathered with pellets removed
For supper they are small and sweet.

ii.

Today a congregation of doves has come
In boisterous praise to the grain fields
Hanging on my porch. I have no gun.
My eyes, as if loaded with birdshot, see
A ritual of fire around a vacant field
And the soft feathers of peace fluttering to earth.

MEMORIAL SERVICE

How long should a moment
Of silence last?
Too short seems
An affront to the moments
Forever gone.
Too long, I know,
Discomforts the silence,
Like stretching time
Beyond its patience.

BOTTOM LINE

Sometimes getting to the bottom of things
The bottom gets to us, and like
A thinking wino we have to admit
The dreams of better don't come true
In the dregs after all the wine is drained,

But move to the next bottle as promises,
Like the viscous film swirled wine leaves.

The bottom assumes a top, as heaven
Needs a hell. Even in the gutter
Of forget we want to believe that wine
Is blood pulsing with light—drink
And behold What-it's-all-about.

But what if

The bottom line is merely acceptance—
The art of beseeching a handout,
A little tithe to purchase one more
Swig of time above the abyss
Where we imagine the bottom lies,

And the space between is all there is.

SISYPHUS MAKING DO

There are times when something as simple
As making a grilled cheese sandwich
Won't work.

The parts are put together—bread, cheese, butter,
Even paprika—but the burner won't start.
The skillet lies there like a lover offering itself.

I change the menu to peanut butter,
Spread profusely on the small, cold surface
Of a Ritz cracker.

THAT'S LIFE, BOYS

Well, well, Bro, Herbie, Chuck, and Deke,
Hammered by how long we've lived,
The news comes like headlines from inside
The scaffolding of failing flesh—
A damned carotid, a congregation of joints
Playing tricks on simple jogs and flashing
Caution at the start of stairs, up or down.

Just yesterday the message appears:
DEKE IS HAVING TWO HERNIAS REPAIRED,
A LIVER BIOPSY, APPENDIX REMOVED,
AND OTHER EXPLORATORY WORK.

Exploration was our playing field, slashing
Through a jungle of ideas, camping out
In philosophical caves, breaking huddle
To charge downfield, waiting on deck
To make the heroic hit—

So Deke's lift has lost its leverage.
We know his liver is juiced with wine.
That superfluous parts are expendable
We intellectually accept.
But pray keep your clinical hands off
That appendage we glory by, that still
Can make our confinement happy, even if
Memory-laden and brain-betrayed.

Now, we wait for the MRI, objects
Of mechanics' tools exploring
The metastasizing assaults of time.

Yet, between being cello sad
And banjo happy, we are still here

Taking our swings: hang in there
Deke, hang in there. Our ailments
Are the nails that hold us together.

000110000011001010110010111110110110010
100000010100110010011011010110000000110
000110001101011 **GODS** 1011010101011101
101011001011100101010110100001011100011
000110000011001010110010111110110110010

GODS

1.
I like to think my hand-me-down brain
Came from the smart ones settling the savannahs
And fishing the Nile, the ones surrendering
To wonder, charting the stars, and setting their days
By the sacred math of the sun. And though
I don't follow their logic of sacrifice or
The letting of blood to bless the wheat,
They did go beyond themselves for gods—
Gods born from the need to eat and the brain's leap
To know from whence we came and whence we go.

2.
The first neuronic conjecture
Sparked inside a poet's brain,
The hallucinatory dream, the music,
Where language birthed a beat, the divine
Refrain hope and fear, the news
An ironic gift from the selfish gene,
Lodged in our reptilian stem.

3.
All the gods moved to myth
When religion turned perpendicular.
Abraham's roots uncrowned the sun
And shamed the shaman. Up turned golden
And Down hotter. Death absolved death.
The singular genius of believe became king
Of legerdemain. From shooting dice to paradise
The future lived in reasons to behave.
Power had a new friend.

4.
My father observed a Sunday Jesus,
My mother added the week. I turned
To signs for relief. When half an arrowhead
Appeared in a 40-acre field the message
Was clear: The missing half was God
Calling me to preach.

5.
I escaped the pulpit and soon left the pew.
Now, I have lower-cased the god of my
Youth. My sister would credit Satan
If she knew. Although I don't believe
I believe all gods can be used.

6.
What do you do for God?
A friend asked.
I look in the mirror.
What do you see?
It is written in us
God saw himself,
But we saw God in us
And praise the reflection.

7.
We believe walking upstairs backwards
As if time did not move ahead.
Purpose is a preacher's shtick,
A stuck needle on an alien sky.
Now we sit in pews of digital salvation.

8.
Hawking might say
Sucked into a black hole we
Could emerge into a new universe
Of multiple selves. Ah, resurrection.

GUCCI JESUS

We are here to measure the Corpse.
Please, please no shapeless shroud.

Leave the arms outstretched for now
The easier to measure for the sleeve.

That loin cloth misleads the waist.
The pants will have to be taken in.

Let's see—from the crotch a normal
Inseam and here is where the cuff will break.

No, no! That raw simple skein won't do.
That's no way to dress a King.

Get me the best imported wool, a tie
Of silk, the latest Roman shirt and shoes.

And clean the dried blood off His feet.
What? Is the Rolex on his bony wrist too much?

No. Prosperity is our faith.
We build the mansions He prepares.

There's no shame in what we sell.
We bring you the Word. It's free.

You simply give what you can.
Can I get an AMEN?

SEARCH AND RESCUE

There was no direct path.
The pines and game-chess thickets
Formed a labyrinth to reach the peak.

From time to time I lost sight
Of its crown, and went to my backpack
For water and bread, saving the wine

For the final ascent. Breaking into
Light beyond the tree line I reached
The peak and absorbed the valley depths

And sky-tipped crown of the opposite range.
Divinity was in the scene. God, I said,
I am here. An echo spoke to me.

For a while I paused to look around
At the mystical formulation
Of valley, mountains and clouds.

Like an echo I returned to level
Ground, gazed up to where I had been
And thanked Bacchus for the wine.

000110000011001010110010111111011011000
100000010100110010011011010110000000110
000001101011110 **ARTIFICE** 101101010110111
011011010111001010101101000010111110001
000110000011001010110010111111011011000

LESSON FROM CÉZANNE

I walk out into the blue
To learn the relativeness of seeing,
The blurred tones of the
Mountain range unfolding
Before my eyes, bursting
Into angles of confusion.
The moment to moment
Shifting of light is ever beyond
My grasp, the shades of color
Too deep for the surface
Of the eye. Up close the fervent
Grass embraces the rocks. A lone
Juniper exclaims the victory
Of roots. How can I ever know
The magnificent space between
The tree and its shadow or stop
The flight in time of the hawk's
Steep dive and the rabbit's terror.
Before I can gather the words,
Knowing they will never
Suffice, everything changes before
My eyes. The question comes again
—is this what I see?

Is the making of art always
The seeing of doubt?

POETRY LESSON

i.

The poem is too accessible, the editor said,
Which I had come to learn meant it was too
Transparent, or more simply, too easy to understand.
(Assuming there was meaning for which to hunt.)
For example, he said, the central image is a tree,
But—well—it appears to remain just a tree.
He was an Eliot/Pound man and at the time I was
Into Billy Collins and the magic of the mundane.
I had spent most of the poem describing the factual
Account of raking the leaves and what I found
Underneath—from a broken creepy doll my daughter
Lost to colonies of bugs I could not name, except for
Ants. He, the editor, had said there was no turn
At the end to make it more than it is. But he
Missed my intent, which is easy to do, especially,
Editors who don't read a poem all the way
Through. The end turned to time as in the autumn
Of my life I imagined when I was gone the leaves
Would continue to fall for the next human to rake.

ii.

As poets are prone to do, so full of self-doubt,
Distrusting even the original muse, I embarked
Upon the inevitable second draft. I created
A stream of sun to spotlight the undressed
Limbs, brought in the music of its roots in concert
With neighbor trees and added the orchestral
Arrangements of the birds that stopped in to sing,
(And even a side comment how at night the tree
Became a nest of stars serenaded by the wind.)
My intent, I think, was to symbolize some sort of
Sacred musical brotherhood, a nature/human duet.

iii.
My wife, the real critic, read the new poem
And was not impressed. Just like a narcissistic
Man, she said, you use the tree to talk about
Yourself. Why not let the tree be a tree. There's
No meaning except what it is. Why not let the tree
Use you. I wasn't sure what she meant, but it
Seemed profound. After my usual creative
Pout, I entered the ring for the third round.

iv.
Less is usually more, and I know the best poems
Are squeezed and squeezed until compressed into
A polished stone that leaks no air, just a solid mass
That reflects. I started pruning until only one word
Was left. Here's the poem now:
                    TREE

v.
For the editor this may not be enough, and probably not
For you. A scientist may claim mis-fired neurons led me astray.
(Or the god-striven failure once again to get inside the truth.)
But the tree is not its name, nor the poem a tree.

vi.
This autumn go out to your favorite tree and rake the leaves,
Then pause and kneel to receive what it gives.

SHOCK OF RECOGNITION

I have found soul-mates in artists
Who live in the narrative I imagine is me.
The work is fabrication of real,
The sieve of purification, searching, digging
For eternal words in the landfill of the brain.

COOL

To borrow an image from Mailer
The criticism of art has ushered in
A robust emptiness between
Two uncertainties. Maybe so.
Maybe that's life.

I still find it better, beyond the
Berets and tenured babble,
To inhale—-hold the words—-
And let the toke take effect.

MR. STEVENS

Is the idea of order a fiction
Of reality made in the eye?
I have been to Key West and watched
The boats move alive with the tide.
Lights blinked on the dark horizon,
Or were they stars?

JIM HARRISON LIVES

Jim Harrison asked "Does Robert Frost
Know he's dead?" Today Jim was found
Dead beside his writing table,
Fingers curved in the shape of his pen,
An unfinished sentence finished now
On a promising sheet of paper, where he lived.

"Jim Harrison do you know you are dead?"
Or are you dreaming of wine-clouded French
Fantasies with three women and a walk
Along the Seine to end with a perfect
Piece of veal drenched in the vérité,
The chef-d'oeuvre,—the gravy.

POETRY FASHION

The buttoned vest and spiffy tie hides
The heart, constricts the throat, flaunts the jeweled
Cuff-links of learned allusions; ransoms the wild
For lecture halls and hors d'oeuvred salons
Where facts of art are framed exhibits.

The cocked hat, the unbuttoned shirt, exposes the heart,
Opens the throat to moan or shout, waves a chest-hair flag
In the face of the bourgeoisie, hangs out
In the Zen glades of spirit to catch the universe's flow,
The next line always open to limitless adornment.

What then does truth wear?
Go deeper beyond the dapper rhyme
Or through the seemingly accidental attire.
The great poem is always naked inside.

RECYCLE

Every afternoon she comes to perform
The Blue Container ritual saying "Excuse me"
In a Spanish accent and quietly empties
Into her trash bag discarded copies
Of stale e-mails, lifeless bureaucratic detritus,
And, frequently, crumpled drafts of a poem

Like this one—

A bagged journey toward new life,
Credit card receipts, directions for kids' games,
Or perhaps the pages of a bright book
That explains how light can be recovered.
(Or, the thought comes, like a bag of wrongs,
Bad love, errant turns, lost schemes.)

It's very possible I'm typing this on new
Waste, the reincarnation of a crumpled up
Chance come back to me

Blank, waiting. . . . .

LOAFING THROUGH DESIGN

for D. C. Berry

There he is walking the branches of the town
            direction random—not lost—but seeking
lostness,   a guide,   *The* guide?

                        to lostness. Yes, my friend, it's a crap shoot out here
            under the clock tower,
a spin-the-bottle game played with the star zoo
                        sky-caged and whirling
                                                down time.

                        All over town church spires wait
            to spear the moon, the night's crown,
beyond the smoke of its haphazard clouds.   Close

                        your eyes and place a blind finger on a verse
            in the Book of Answers; open your eyes and read:
take this street and you'll be found.   Promises.   Promises.

                        Or head where the bottle points to the night-swirling
            roulette wheel of astrocreatures: Pisces: you will
meet a virgin tonight but beware the Crab. O,   universal

                        punster would-be poet drawing pictures from where God, *god?*
            banged the stars,   stalker, hunter, Venus-hound lusting after
what the stamen knows
                        centered in its circle of perfect petals.

                        He can figure the odds of she loves me
she loves me not.   He knows gravity does not gamble.
                        But no one knows what silicon glint
            off the moonstruck sidewalk will catch his eye.
The largest and smallest things stumble through the poet's math.

He circles the square, goes round its axis of justice and concludes
      for tonight there's no need to make the best case to the jury.
         What's the best case?

        Guilty or not guilty he happens to be here   here
    is as good a place as any to watch insidious Cancer skulk across the light-
polluted sky   the moon depart
            and the sun rise in brightening salutation

to the cross-signed dogwood, its beauty blazing in his eyes.

CAGE

My house has glass that lets the outside
In. I can look out and see metaphors
Hanging in the palms, floating in the pool,
Swimming through the canal out to Clam Bay,
The Gulf of Mexico, the Atlantic, Europe,
China, and all the way back around to
The west coast of Florida and my chair.

Today I am watching another bird,
A cardinal, that has entered the lanai
Through the hole in the screen the last
Hurricane made. Panicked in its accidental cage,
It does not understand freedom lies
In going out the way it came in.

Settle down and rest awhile, I say.
You will soon learn the trick of knowing
That entrance and exit are the same.

PAUL

The VW Bug became the RoachmoBeetle
When we took our tokes on the Columbus
Back roads, paranoia a tightening noose
Around our gothic musings. The sweet
Smell arose out of the Odor of Verbena.
Quentin committed suicide so Faulkner
Didn't have to. The South was all fiction,
Lies toward the truth. And, you ask,
What about the King James Bible, and I say
Ain't that the truth. Remember it was you
Who put a pair of rednecks on Noah's Ark
To practice their love of Bar-b-Que.

Pasture football was our high on Sundays,
Adolescent men playing the hut-hut
Of fumbled dreams. The Yankee scout said
My college curve ball was the best he had seen,
Before the elbow blew. Your fullback
Heart was betrayed by treacherous knees.
Not sure when, but one of us spoke
"Well, sheeit. Let's take our marijuana IQs
And git Pee Aitch Dees."

Which we did. But now I'm not sure how
To end this poem. The note to me said "passed away,"
But that's not you. You were a handy-man,
Prolific in all forms, the Poet Laureate of all of Texas.

Did I miss something beneath the banter of our last exchange—
The running graveyard humor about your skills on
The hand controls of your Rollators, one
In every room now, or the artist neurosurgeon
Who advised against restructuring your spine ("screws
And rods and all that shit") that probably wouldn't help you

Walk again and the pain would be worse? "Put yer knives
Up," you said. "I guess I'm stuck with this crap. . . ."

The upbeat was the gun book news, the beauty and truth
Of the BAR 1918A3 and M240 SLR.
"The M240 is 7.62 NATO, belt-fed, and I get
A kick out of watching that belt feed out of the can
And into that damned thing. It kicks the cases straight
Down and the links out the side, so you don't have
To scrabble around all over the place picking up empties."

The last time there you showed me your arsenal,
Locked and loaded, ready for the militia crazies. The end
You prepared for was Armageddon, not passing away.

You explained my paltry Ruger: Double-action revolvers
Are those that can be fired by merely pulling the trigger
And by cocking and pulling the trigger, whereas single-
Actions are those that have to be cocked before being fired.
They work better if you want to put it against your temple.
You have one of those Ruger Single Sixes, which
Have a .22 Long Rifle cylinder and a .22 Magnum cylinder.
"Damned fine little pistols. I've had several over the years."

It was my sister's funeral that led us back to death.
"Gawd, I hate funerals. I ain't even going to my own: gon'
Be cremated and have my ashes shot out of shotgun shells
In different places that I have over the years developed
A fondness for. The toughest part will be trying to teach
Amber how to load the damned things. We'll practice
With wood ashes or something, you know, since it'd
Be kinda hard to teach her how to load my own. . . ."

A good plan, my friend. We started with ashes.

00011000001100101011001011111011011000
10000001010011001001101101011000000110
00000110101101 10 **OTHER** 10110101010111101
10101011101100101010110100001011110001
00011000001100101011001011111011011000

WILLIAM

The dictionary in your brain
Has the word "apraxia,"
But you cannot open the pages.

The alphabet is there too, pristine,
But you cannot sing a, b, c, d,
E, f, g, h, i, j, k, l, m, n, o, p,
Q, r, s, t, u, v, w, x, y, and z.

Now I know my A, B, Cs, next time
Won't you sing with me.

I sing and exaggerate the sounds,
Coaxing you to repeat.
You record but do not sing along.

Instead your mouth and throat make
The sound (unt, unh) that stands
For everything,

That unconnected to your brain says,
Sing it again, and once more I make

Those sounds so taken for granted.
I know they enter the cells of your knowing,
And I wait, wait for your mouth

To call them out, waiting to hear
That golden palindrome I keep
Saying for you to repeat: D.A.D.

ANNIVERSARY POEM

for Jodi

I can tell by your breathing that you
        Have left our bed,
Your mind sleep-walking to whatever
        Memory called you away,
Perhaps back on the river in Humble,
        The pig-tailed tomboy
Flying out on the rope swing.
        Maybe you went back to Cape
Coral shattered by your father's death.
        Or you've gone to your office.
In a mysterious fog it keeps moving away
        Every time you try to go in.
Before bed we had watched *Road House*
        Again. Taking my hand and
Stroking my face you swooned as usual
        Over Sam Elliot's voice and gait.
And we made love on the couch.

Looking at your face shrouded
        In the rich corn shock of hair
I go to my waking dream of our living past:
        The day we went to the Uffizi
And stood in holiness before Botticelli's
        Painting of you. That night
You stepped out of the frame and came
        To me as if floating on a half shell.
Those moments were the chisel marks
        Michelangelo made freeing the slaves
From their marble cells. Freed from our pasts
        We were free to make our own.

Dreams rummage through the archives
       Of our brains, pick us up and take us away,
To places familiar and strange. We go but
       Never stay. In the morning we will turn
To each other, kiss and embrace. I will say
       "Happy anniversary, my love." Jessi
And William will come in with the card they made.
       I will start the music box that
Has Venus on the lid, and let it play. For dinner
       We will open the bottle of Chianti
And toast another year of love that gives meaning
       To our past every day.

SANIBEL

for Jeff

The roses had no knowledge of the purchase,
Or that death deserves to leave with beauty,
(Yet, they were beautiful)
Or that they would honor ashes—
A floating armada of momentary grief
And lasting memory of letting go.

All morning the cluttering rain questioned
Our departure, the boats clustered around
The marina like a gathering of sand pipers,
Waiting gulls, and wealthy herons.

When the sun let us go the diesel could
Have thought it was a normal day,
Churning the prop out through the channel
Into the open Gulf, another pleasure hunt
For dolphins, iPhones alert for awe.

Three miles out the difference was exposed.
Engine doused, soft waves interceded
With the ferryman on behalf of the freed soul.

The offering of roses shone in the sun
Until we could see them no more.
Our eyes turned to the dolphins leaping
Through our wake, brief arcs of joy,
The sea saying the play goes on.

THE NOUNS GO FIRST

In Memoriam for Ralph

As we walked the beach, waiting
For the sun to set—

The nouns go first, you said,
And pointed to the sand slowly
Feeding the waves.
Even the sandpipers stood
Like feathered nouns
                    Ready to fly away.

A cloud of stingrays moved
Just out of reach, then
Disappeared
Into seaweed murk the sudden
Surf made.

Coquina shells tumbled in like
Memories, their destiny to float out
With the moon's sway.

Everything with a name
Leaves.
Be awed, you said.
            Remember as long as you can.
Your thank-you note came
With a list of all the nouns we
Encountered on the beach that day
As we stood
And watched the sunset pull
            The light away.

I remember all I can, the easy ones
Like Twilight. Shells. Tide. Seaspray.
But, old friend, if nouns go first

Love is the last noun that stays.

BLESSING

For Valerie and Joe—Wedding day—October 5, 2020

Amor wears many masks of mythic appeal:
The once-upon-a-time-happy-ever-after tale,
The romantic rose wet with the dew of spring,
The old belief in marriage of the eyes,
Or the fateful wound of Cupid's arrowed aim.
Add to these
The promised truth that lies in sacred vows
And the alchemical mix of two becoming one.

So what dear muse do you see for us?

Let's say two hearts entwined in equal parts,
Framed in partnership of trust, passion, and joy,
Enduring like a masterpiece of art;
Two bodies anointed with blessings of touch
And the honesty of skin;
Two minds together, friends when apart.

Two in love is a blessing
Two minds nurture
And hearts feel.

Here's to two hearts
Having come together
To make the blessing real,
And to a match blessed with the spark
By which the spirit of love
Forever lives.

WEST TEXAS SUMMER DAY

For Walt McDonald

i.
The sun is salt on a slug;
Flesh foams,
Muscles snap like dry-rotted
Rubber bands
And dust sops
The blood:
In the wind's dry throat
Bones debate
The permanence of ashes.

ii.
Late afternoon
Pulls down a vermilion haze:
Bleached bones cool back to blood,
Sinews plait their strength
Into flesh and spirit unclenches
In the wind's breath:
A prolonged corpse
Sings

NEWS FROM THE LIVING ROOM:

A Note Found to a Relative in Vietnam

The once unpronounceable names for the American tongue,
   Phuoc Ben, Khe Sanh, Phnom Penh,
      Are easier to say now. Today,
In that giraffeneck shaped land, I saw a young soldier's
   Pimpled face explode in blood,
      His acne cured by a satchel charge.
I could have turned it off or not watched
   But I wanted something to say
      To you about the war.
The blood ran down the wall and we can't get it off the carpet.

It was said the cameraman vomited when
   They washed the boy's
      Brains away with a hose.
I could have turned it off and made a game out of
   Touching the dial without
      Getting blood on my hand,
But the cameraman got sick and that surprised me
   Because you'd think they would
      Be accustomed to that.
The daily casualties are now totaled and announced flatly at the
                                                end of the week.

This week it was 225 dead; 1230 wounded or missing.
   That's about all I have to say.
      I could have turned
It off and maybe saved the carpet. Some very good
   Programs are coming on: GREEN ACRES,
      HOGAN'S HEROES.
Tonight's movie is THE SANDS OF IWO JIMA.
   And all the talk shows—all the beautiful people—
      They always say
Such funny things. That's about all I have to say. I could have
                                                turned it off.

97

CATCHING A STRAY DOG NEAR WHITEVILLE, N.C.

It strayed from her faith and his instinct
It could be kept—

Strange eyes trusting no stranger,
Watching for its life among savage wheels,

Dead to commands, its razor bones
Seeking a god through feasts of dust.

It had happened before, her faith
That she could tame and bring home

Whatever slept wild and homeless
Beneath dark porches.

And so he waited, pulled, feeling her
Holding out herself to what

Was hanging back suspicious and amazed,
Its hunger too strong to long doubt

The kneeled gesture, beseeching,
Submitting to it her faith in connections.

It came—instinct and faith,
Mouth to hand,

Proof, for the moment, against strangeness,
A picture of family.

THE CYBORG AND THE POET

It started with trouble in the skull
That made the poems more efficient
And precise, but so pathologically uptight:
You possess a head computerized.
You perceive through newer eyes.
You comprehend the old you lost
By computing correctly total cost.

And progressed to a defective heart
That moiling for the old mastery
Fell into the arrhythmia of memory loss:
My heart leaps up and stalls
For a thing of beauty is a joy that palls.
Something there is that doesn't love a fable,
Or patient evenings etherized upon a table.

ELEGY

Strange craft had flown in his mind.
His heart was bent on giving names
To unidentified flying objects
Of supremely human things. Now
His blood efficiently floods the Dacron
Arteries of a plastic heart,
And so that the skeleton might
Support the parts they put in ceramic
Joints and metallic bones. The
Cyborg has healed and gone home.
The poet stays, heaped, used head,
Malfunctioned heart, old bones tied
With dried veins, anachronistic,
Obsolete, victim of disease, and death.

ABOUT THE AUTHOR

The Algorithm of I is Jack Crocker's second collection of poems. The first, *The Last Resort*, was published in 2009 by the Texas Review Press. His poems have appeared in *The Texas Review, Southern Poetry Review, Mississippi Review,* and other journals, with fiction in *The Cimarron Review.* Poems have been anthologized in *The Texas Anthology; Mississippi Writers: Reflections of Childhood; Texas Stories and Poems; and Florida in Poetry.* He scripted and performed "Introduction to Folksongs" for Mississippi Educational Television that was aired nationally. An interview was chosen by Galway Kinnell to be included in *Walking Down Stairs.* A biography of Jimmy Rodgers was published in *Mississippi Heroes* and of Sergeant York in *Heroes of Tennessee.* He has written songs for StaFree Publishing Company and had a recording contract with Fretone Records of Memphis, Tennessee. Having received college scholarships for basketball and baseball, he is Dean Emeritus of Florida Gulf Coast University, and currently professor of English and provost and executive vice president of academic affairs at Western New Mexico University.